Knitting Lace Triangles

by Evelyn A. Clark

Published by Fiber Trends, Inc.
www.fibertrends.com

ISBN 1-933398-01-9

Photographer
Joe Galeskas

Editor
Bev Galeskas

First published in 2007 by
Fiber Trends, Inc.
315 Colorado Park Place
East Wenatchee, WA 98802
www.fibertrends.com

Printed in the USA
Classic Printing
East Wenatchee, WA

Introduction

Lace can be surprisingly simple and fun to knit. Because the results often are so spectacular, though, it can appear intimidating. In the case of the Flower, Leaf, Medallion and Ripple lace in this book, appearances are deceiving. Although they are beautiful and interesting enough for experts, they are designed to be simple enough for knitters new to lace. These small patterns repeat over 10 stitches, so they are easy to memorize and look great in a variety of yarns. They can be used alone or combined to create an endless array of triangular scarves and shawls.

Why triangles? Visionary R. Buckminster Fuller called triangles the basic building blocks of the universe. He might not have been talking about lace triangles, but they are a basic in the knitting world. Shaping is simple and starts with a few stitches at the neck that increase in a chevron shape to the scalloped edging. This edging can be started at the end of any lace repeat, making it easy to customize the size and accommodate the amount of yarn on hand.

Also, lace triangles are versatile accessories. They can be knit in a variety of fibers and colors, as well as tweed, heather and glitzy yarns. Smaller sizes can be worn as scarves with a jeans jacket or business ensemble. Larger sizes make elegant shawls for formal functions or cozy wraps for relaxing at home.

Best of all, they provide comforting warmth and make a wonderful gift to show that, as an old song says, "I love you a bushel and a peck and a hug around the neck." Whether you are creating a hug for yourself or someone else, I hope you have as much fun knitting lace triangles as I have had creating this book.

Evelyn A. Clark

Sunshine and Shadows Shawl -
Garter Leaf, Medallion and Ripple lace
in fingering weight

Table of Contents

Designing Lace Triangles

This book is organized to help knitters design their own triangle using four simple laces -- Flower, Leaf, Medallion and Ripple. Each lace can be used alone or combined with any or all of the others. After a description of these lace patterns, other design options are listed.

A single-lace triangle requires little planning. For multi-lace triangles, the patterning can be planned or worked randomly. Either way, it is helpful to understand how to use transition rows and create a pattern outline. After discussing how to select materials, read charts, correct mistakes and join yarns, four cast-ons are described. Both written instructions and charts are included for the lace patterns and edging. The Size and Yardage Chart in the Appendix shows yarn requirements and triangle sizes for four weights of yarn.

The shawls shown throughout the book are described in the Appendix. Whether these are used as a template or an inspiration, a great way to plan a design is to think about what it can represent. Personalizing it with a story can offer comfort, celebrate an accomplishment, commemorate a special occasion or express a dream for the future. Flowers can represent beauty, hope and renewal; leaves can represent growth and change and ripples can represent waves in the river of life or the passing of time. The names of the motifs are very general to inspire a variety of possibilities. Thinking about what the lace can represent when planning and knitting the triangle gives it special meaning. Use your imagination, and write out a story to keep or give with a gift.

"The universe is made of stories, not atoms." - Muriel Rukeyser

Anatomy of the Triangle -

Triangles in this book start with a few stitches at the neck and increase to a scalloped edge. The advantages of this design are that the lace begins on few stitches, the lace patterning forms interesting chevron bands and the edging can be started at the end of any lace pattern repeat.

The diagram below shows the basic parts of the triangle.

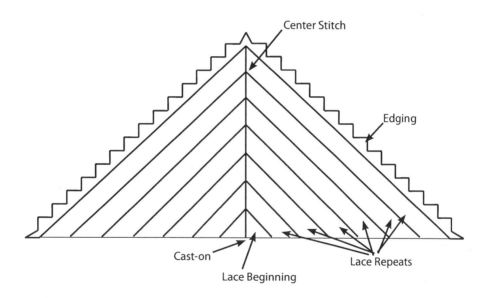

As shown, the triangle really is two triangles, separated by a center stitch. This means that the lace patterning for the first half of a row simply is repeated after the center stitch for the second half of the row.

Medallion Shawl -
Stockinette Medallion lace
in sport weight

Knitting Lace

The key to lace knitting is a hole made with a yarn-over. This is an increased stitch -- remember the holes in beginners' knitting and resulting increase in stitches? Therefore, the yarn-over must be accompanied by a decrease unless it is used for shaping. Yarn-overs link up to create the lace motifs, and a great way to see how they do this is a chart. So charts, as well as written instructions, are included for the lace.

The Flower, Leaf, Medallion and Ripple lace used for the triangles in this book have patterning only on odd numbered rows, and the triangle shaping is included in this patterning.

Each lace can be used alone or combined with any or all of the others.

"Adventure is worthwhile in itself." - Amelia Earheart

Flower Lace -

The most open pattern, it repeats over 10 stitches and 10 rows. This lace can represent roses, peonies or any other favorite flower.

Leaf Lace -

The most solid of the laces, this is a traditional pattern from the Shetland Islands. It biases, which means the stitches slant because the decreases are not next to the yarn-overs, and this creates interesting patterning with multi-colored yarns. This lace can represent leaves from any tree, as well as trees, fir cones or feathers. It repeats over 10 stitches and 10 rows.

Medallion Lace -

This lace features traditional Shetland Island cat's paw lace inside an undulating pattern. It can represent bubbles, sand dollars, paw prints, daisies, forget-me-nots or other flowers, and it also repeats over 10 stitches and 10 rows.

Ripple Lace -

Instead of undulating vertically like the other three laces, this pattern zig zags horizontally. Ripples can represent sunshine, water, evergreens, mountain tops or waves of energy. It repeats over 10 stitches and 20 rows.

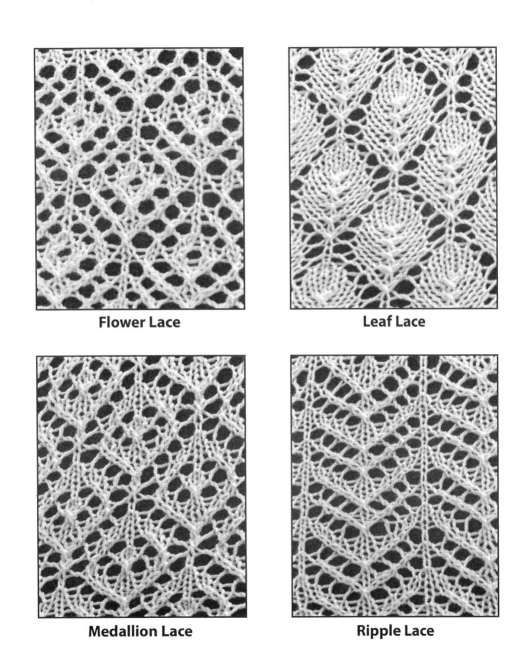

Flower Lace

Leaf Lace

Medallion Lace

Ripple Lace

Design Options

The four lace patterns in this book were designed to offer a variety of options for knitting a triangle.

One Lace or More -
A single lace can be used, or it can be combined with the other laces. Changes can be made regularly, randomly or just once such as for a bottom border before the Edging. (See photo of Stockinette Stitch Swatch, page 16.)

Clear or Subtle Changes -
Changing from one lace to another at the end of a Repeat creates interesting chevron bands of lace. (See photo of Rose Ribbons Shawl, page 57.) If a more subtle change is preferred, Transition rows can be substituted for the final rows of a Repeat to allow one lace to flow into the next.

Stockinette or Garter Stitch -
The lace can be knit in stockinette stitch, which has a right side and a wrong side, or garter stitch, which is reversible and requires no purling.
(See photos of Stockinette and Garter Stitch Swatches, pages 16 and 17.)

Plain or Beaded Scallops -
One or three beads can be added at the Edging to accent the scalloped points. (See photos of beaded scallops at right.)

1 Bead per Scallop

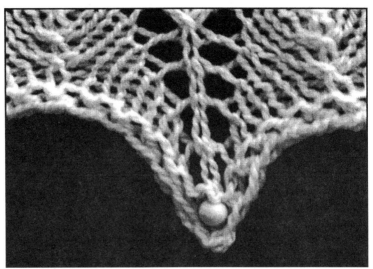

3 Beads per Scallop

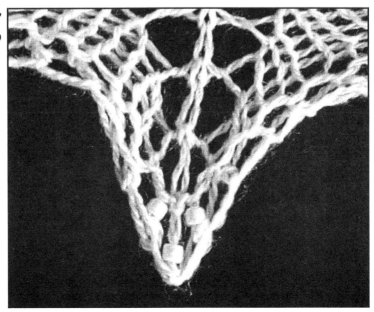

Smooth Yarn Sample- Garden Shawl in silk and wool lace weight knit in stockinette stitch lace

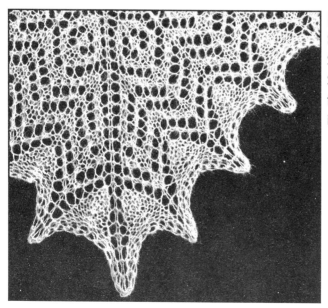

Fuzzy Yarn Sample- Sunshine and Shadows Shawl in suri alpaca fingering weight knit in garter stitch lace

Yarns -

The triangles can be made from a variety of handspun or commercial yarns in lace to worsted weights. Since the lace motifs are small and repeat regularly, they show up well in multi-colored, tweed, heather, fuzzy and glitzy yarns, as well as solid-color, smooth yarns.

Single or Multiple Colors -

In addition to using multi-colored yarns, more than one solid color can be used in a triangle to create chevrons of color patterning. Colors can be changed when the lace changes or periodically within one lace.

Sizes -

Because the Edging can be started at the end of any lace Repeat, it is easy to customize the size. The Size and Yardage Chart on pages 60 and 61 shows 12 alternatives for each of four weights of yarn based on the sample shawls in this book.

"If you always do what interests you, at least one person is pleased." - Katherine Hepburn

Stockinette Stitch Swatch

Medallion with other lace

Medallion with Leaf Border

Medallion with Flower Border

Medallion with Ripple Border

Medallion only

Garter Stitch Swatch

Ripple with other lace

Ripple with Leaf Border

Ripple with Flower Border

Ripple only

Ripple with Medallion Border

Planning a Triangle

Every triangle starts with a lace Beginning after the cast-on. The Beginning for each lace is worked over 18 rows and starts both the lace patterning and the triangle shaping.

The Beginning is followed by 10-row Repeats for Flower, Leaf and Medallion lace or 20-row Repeats for Ripple lace. Each triangle ends with an 8-row Edging. Because the Edging is the same for all the triangles, the Beginning and the Repeats are the components that make up the design.

Changes in the lace can be made after the Beginning and after any Repeat. These changes will create a line like the edge of a ribbon except between Medallion and Ripple lace, which flow together. This line is most distinct between Flower and Leaf lace as shown on the Rose Ribbons Shawl at right. The lace will flow together without the ribbon effect if Transition rows are knit before changing lace patterns.

Transition Rows -

Transition rows combine the motifs of two lace patterns to create a seamless flow from one to another. These 4-row patterns can be substituted for the last 4 rows of a Beginning or Repeat.

Because the last 4 rows of both Medallion and Ripple lace are the same, they naturally flow together, and no Transition is needed as shown on the Sand Dollar Shawl, page 23.

For all other lace changes to flow together, Transition rows must be used.

Instructions and charts are included for five Transition patterns. The written instructions for each lace Repeat lists the Transition patterns that can be used before starting that lace. Transition rows also are used before the Edging except for Leaf lace, which naturally flows into the Edging.

**Garden Shawl with Transition rows
between Flower and Leaf lace**

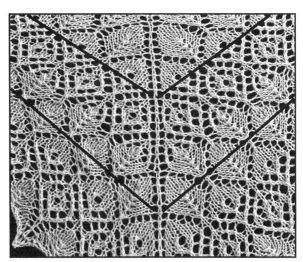

**Rose Ribbons Shawl with no Transition
rows between Flower and Leaf lace**

Using the Size and Yardage Chart

The Size and Yardage Chart in the Appendix shows the number of stitches and rows needed for a variety of sizes of triangles in four weights of yarn. The Rows-to-Edging numbers at the top of the chart are the easiest to use when planning a triangle. Below are two ways to use them.

One option is to choose a size for the triangle and a yarn weight. Then look at the top of the chart to find the Rows-to-Edging number. Subtract the 18 Beginning rows from that number, and the remaining number can be divided into 10-row and 20-row Repeats to plan the lace design. Remember to include the Beginning lace in the overall design.

A second method is to start with a choice of lace patterns, adding increments of 10 rows for Flower, Leaf and Medallion lace or 20 rows for Ripple lace. One lace will be the Beginning, so add those 18 rows for the total. On the Size and Yardage Chart, look down the column for that Rows-to-Edging number to select a yarn and triangle size.

Single-Lace Triangles -

Little planning is needed for triangles with one lace. Simply select a cast-on, start the lace with the Beginning and continue with the Repeats until 4 rows before the Edging. Then substitute the 4 rows of Transition 1 for the last 4 rows of the Flower, Medallion and Ripple lace Repeats, and knit the Edging.
For Leaf lace, no Transition is needed; just work desired number of Repeats, and then start the Edging.

The number of Repeats can be calculated from the Size and Yardage Chart Rows-to-Edging number as shown in the following examples:

Flower, Leaf or Medallion Triangle		Ripple Triangle
Desired Rows-to-Edging	108	118
Less Beginning rows	-18	-18
Remaining rows	90	100
10-row Repeat = 9 Repeats		20-row Repeat = 5 Repeats

For Ripple lace, the number remaining after the 18 Beginning rows must be divisible by 20. These numbers are marked with an asterisk on the Size and Yardage Chart.

Multi-Lace Triangles With Random Changes -

Triangles with 2 or more lace patterns also can be worked with little planning. If a ribbon effect is preferred, simply cast on, knit a Beginning and then work Repeats, changing lace when desired.
For seamless changes from one lace to the next, look at the written instructions for the next Repeat to find the necessary Transition rows. Substitute those rows for the last 4 rows of lace being completed.

21

Multi-Lace Triangles with Planned Changes -

The examples below show how to calculate lace changes for a triangle where the lace alternates with every Repeat. (See Sand Dollar Shawl, at right.) Ripple lace is included since it has the larger 20-row Repeat and shows how the placement of lace patterns affects the rows required.

Ripple Beginning	18 Rows
10-Row Medallion Repeat + 20-Row Ripple Repeat	30 Rows

(No Transition rows needed except before Edging)

       30-row repeat worked 3x (90) + Beginning (18) = 108 Rows-to-Edging

Therefore, a triangle with 108 Rows-to-Edging can be made with a Ripple Beginning and three alternating Medallion and Ripple Repeats. (This same number works for a Medallion Beginning and three alternating Ripple and Medallion Repeats.) However, if the sequence shown above ends with another Medallion Repeat, 118 Rows-to-Edging would be needed to accommodate the extra 10-row Repeat.

If the lace patterning is changed to a Medallion Beginning (18 rows) and three alternating Ripple and Medallion Repeats (90 rows) plus a final Ripple Repeat (20 rows) the Rows-to-Edging required would change to 128.

All of the examples above use alternating Ripple and Medallion Repeats, but the numbers change based on the sequence of the patterns. This is important to remember when planning a triangle that includes Ripple lace.

"Ever since I was a little girl, I always wanted to be somebody.
Now I see I should have been more specific." - Lily Tomlin

Sand Dollar Shawl -
Stockinette Medallion and Ripple lace
in worsted weight

Sunshine and Shadows Shawl -
Garter Leaf, Medallion and Ripple lace
in fingering weight

Creating a Pattern Outline

When planning a design, it is helpful to list all of the rows, including any Transition rows. Following is an example of a plan for the Sunshine and Shadows garter stitch shaw with Medallion and Leaf lace alternating to a Ripple border. Transition rows are substituted for the final 4 rows of the Beginning and each Repeat except between Medallion and Ripple Border where no Transition is needed.

Medallion Beginning	
including Transition 1	18 rows
*Leaf Repeat	
including Transition 3	10 rows
Medallion Repeat	
including Transition 1	10 rows
Repeat from * 2 more times, ending with	
Medallion Repeat	
no Transition needed	40 rows
Ripple Repeat	
including Transition 1	<u>20 rows</u>
Total Rows-to-Edging	98 rows

After outlining a plan, photocopy the written instructions and/or charts for the Beginning, each Repeat and each Transition that will be used.
These sections can be cut and taped or pasted onto one sheet for easy reference.

"Reality is something you rise above." - Liza Minnelli

Materials and Supplies

Yarns -

These lace triangles can be made from handspun or commercial yarns of almost any weight. Try them in lace, fingering, Shetland/sport/dk or aran/worsted weights.

Lace also looks great in a variety of natural fibers, such as alpaca, bamboo, cashmere, cotton, mohair, silk and wool, as well as man-made fibers. For yarn yardage requirements, see Size and Yardage Charts on pages 60 & 61.

Note: Acrylic yarns can be used, but because they are created with memory to spring back to their original size, they will not hold a blocked shape unless they are heavily steamed to set the new shape permanently.

Needles -

Because the triangles are knit in a chevron shape, circular needles work best. Lengths of 24" to 32" (60 to 80 cm) are good for all except large triangles in heavier yarns when a longer needle is helpful.

Choose a needle 2 - 4 sizes larger than recommended for the yarn.

Gauge -

For a swatch, cast on 20 - 30 sts, and knit for a few inches in plain stockinete or garter stitch. Take swatch off needles, pull in all directions to relax the stitches and then smooth out. The gauge should be loose enough for swatch to drape without the stitches looking stringy. If preferred, the shawl beginning can substitute for a gauge swatch. After working a cast-on and a lace Beginning, stretch the piece to see how the stitches will look after blocking. They should not be so loose or tight that the yarn-over patterning does not show. Other than that, it is a matter of personal preference. If it looks good, keep going. If not, change needles and start over.

Additional Supplies -

2 stitch markers to mark center stitch and ending border

A coilless pin to hang at side edge to mark beginning of odd numbered rows

Sharp-pointed sewing needle with eye large enough to accommodate yarn

Rust-proof pins for blocking

Tape measure

Optional Supplies -

Crochet hook and several yards of smooth, contrasting colored waste yarn for a provisional cast-on

Blocking wires

Beads with holes large enough to accommodate yarn, and a crochet hook small enough to fit through the hole of the bead. Number of beads needed is included on the Size and Yardage Chart on pages 60 and 61.

Note: Test beads for colorfastness before using.

Chart Symbols and Abbreviations

Only six basic knitting techniques are used to create the lace. Following are the chart symbols, abbreviations and definitions for those techniques:

Chart Symbol	Abbreviation	Definition
☐	k	Knit
*N/A	p	Purl
/	k2tog	Knit 2 stitches together as one
\	ssk	(Slip, slip, knit) Slip 1 stitch knitwise, slip the next stitch knitwise, place those 2 sts back on holding needle and knit them together through the back loops
/\	sk2p	Slip 1 stitch knitwise, knit 2 stitches together and pass slipped stitch over k2tog stitch
O	yo	(Yarn over) Bring yarn forward between the needles then back over the top of needle before working the next stitch

*No chart symbol for purl since purl only is used on even numbered (WS) rows for stockinette stitch lace, and even numbered rows are not charted.

Additional Abbreviations Used -

RS	Right side of triangle
WS	Wrong side of triangle
inc	Increase 1 by knitting in the front and then the back of a stitch
st or sts	Stitch or stitches
* *	Repeat instructions between the asterisks
[ ]	Repeat instructions within brackets up to the stitches indicated
x	Times
wpi	Wraps per inch

Wraps Per Inch -

This is a measurement often used for handspun yarns where yarn is wrapped around a ruler, dowel or pencil for one inch and the wraps are counted.

Wraps should be done without stretching the yarn.

See Size and Yardage Chart for yarn categories.

Note that often these will differ from yarn label information, which is okay. This is just a measurement to track personal knitting style and preferences.

Special Tips

Reading Charts -

Charts show how the yarn-overs link up to create the lace patterns. They are read from bottom to top and from right to left. For charts showing a center stitch, start with the 2 border stitches; then work across to the center stitch. For the second half of the row, again read chart from right to left, ignoring the 2 border stitches and working them at the end instead of the center stitch. Only odd rows are charted, and all even rows to the last Edging row can be worked as k2, purl to last 2 sts, k2 for stockinette stitch lace or simply knit for garter stitch lace. Cast-on, final Edging rows and cast-off are included in the written instructions.

Counting Rows -

When knitting lace, it is easy to lose track of how many rows have been worked. Fortunately, there is a very easy way to calculate this. Complete a wrong side row, count the total stitches, subtract 7 (the cast-on stitches) and divide the resulting number by 2.

For example, if there are 187 stitches, subtracting 7 stitches and dividing the remainder by 2 means that 90 rows have been completed.

Correcting Mistakes -

If the stitch count is off, it is easiest to look at the yarn-overs to discover where the mistake occurred. A missing yarn-over can be created one or two rows later simply by lifting the bar between the stitches of the appropriate row to create the yarn-over and weaving it up to the current row. To eliminate an extra yarn-over, simply take it off the needles and unravel it. The slight looseness in the tension will not show after blocking.

"Mistakes are part of the dues one pays for a full life." - Sophia Loren

Joining Yarns -

Because lace is open, it is difficult to hide yarn tails when a new ball of yarn is started. A great way to overcome this problem is the Sewn Splice. Thread new yarn into a sharp-pointed needle. Beginning approximately an inch from the end of old yarn, run the needle in and out of the old yarn towards the knitting for about 2 inches. Pull the end of the new yarn through the sewn section of the old yarn, leaving a second inch of tail. Rub sewn section of doubled yarn between your palms to smooth. Resume knitting and trim yarn ends after blocking. Using this method to join yarns will leave only the beginning and ending tails to weave in after the shawl is knit.

Sewn Splice

If switching colors, use Looped Sewn Splice. Loop yarn, sew tail back into same yarn but do not pull loop closed. Thread new yarn into needle, run through loop of old yarn and then sew new yarn tail into new yarn. Pull yarn ends to close loops, but leave tails to trim after blocking.

Looped Sewn Splice

Casting On

The lace in the triangle is framed by a 2-stitch garter border that starts with the cast-on and continues at the beginning and end of every row. This border can be started with a Garter Stitch Tab or any ordinary cast-on.

Garter Stitch Tab -

The advantage of starting with this cast-on is that the garter stitch ridges flow naturally into the borders. It starts with 2 stitches that are knit into a narrow garter stitch rectangle. On the last row the tab is rotated to knit stitches along three sides as described below.

Following are three ways to make this tab.

> 1. Crocheted Chain Provisional Cast-on: Using a crochet hook and a smooth waste yarn, chain 4. Using shawl yarn and knitting needles, knit up 2 sts in 2 of the bumps on the back of the chain.
> Rows 1 - 6: Knit.
> Row 7: k2, pick up and knit 1 st in each of 3 garter ridges along side of shawl yarn tab; unzip waste yarn chain, put 2 shawl yarn sts onto needles and knit those 2 sts. (7 sts)
>
> 2. Waste Yarn Beginning:
> With smooth waste yarn and knitting needles, cast on 2 stitches.
> Rows 1 - 4: Knit.
> Row 5: Change to shawl yarn and k2.
> Rows 6 - 10: Knit.
> Row 11: k2, pick up and knit 1 st in each of 3 garter ridges along side edge of shawl yarn tab; carefully cut away waste yarn sts, put 2 shawl yarn sts onto needles and knit those 2 sts. (7 sts)

3. Backwards Loop Cast-on: With knitting needle and shawl yarn, loosely cast on 2 sts by putting 2 backwards loops on needle.

Rows 1 - 6: Knit.

Row 7: k2, pick up and knit 1 st in each of 3 garter stitch ridges along side edge of tab and k2 in top loops of beginning cast-on. (7 sts)

Garter Stitch Tab Beginning

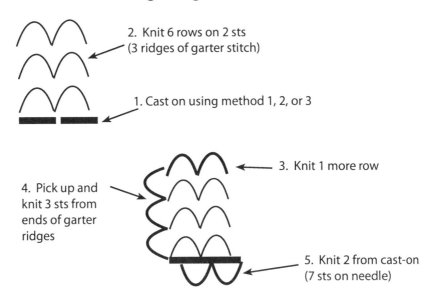

2. Knit 6 rows on 2 sts
(3 ridges of garter stitch)

1. Cast on using method 1, 2, or 3

3. Knit 1 more row

4. Pick up and knit 3 sts from ends of garter ridges

5. Knit 2 from cast-on
(7 sts on needle)

Ordinary Cast-On -

Instead of the Garter Stitch Tab, any ordinary cast-on can be used.

With the shawl yarn and needles, cast on 5 sts.

Rows 1 & 2: Knit.

Row 3: k1, inc 1 (knit in front and back of st), k1, inc 1, k1. (7 sts)

Row 4: Knit.

"The secret of getting ahead is getting started." - Sally Berger

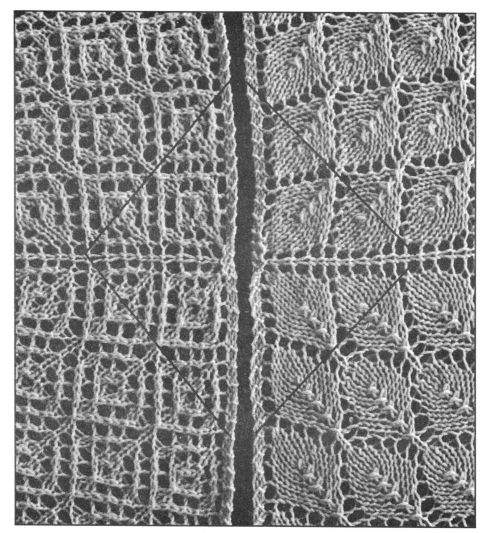

Flower and Leaf Shawl Beginnings -
Lines mark the end of the 18-row Beginnings
Medallion and Ripple Beginnings are shown
on the square swatches on pages 16 & 17

Lace Beginnings

If the triangle has not been planned, now is the time to pick a lace for the 18-row Beginning. This lace can be used once, for several Repeats or throughout. To switch to a different lace immediately after the Beginning, see Transition Information in the written instructions for the Repeat of the next lace.

It also is the time to decide if the lace will be knit in stockinette stitch or garter stitch. (See Photos of Stockinette and Garter Stitch Swatches, pages 16 and 17.)

Note: Directions are written for stockinette stitch. If garter stitch lace is preferred, knit all even rows.

The triangles increase 4 stitches every other row to the Edging. These yarn-over increases are included in the lace patterning and are worked on either side of the center stitch and inside each of the garter stitch borders.

Like the lace patterning, the increases are worked only on odd numbered (RS) rows. It is helpful to place stitch markers before the center stitch and before the ending border and to hang a coilless safety pin along the side edge to mark the start of odd numbered rows.

Each shawl begins with an 18-row Beginning that can be worked from the written instructions or charts.

Flower Lace Beginning: (Chart 1)

Row 1: (RS) k2, *yo, k1, yo, place marker,* k1, repeat between *s, k2. (11 sts)

Row 2 and all even rows: (WS) k2, purl to last 2 sts, k2.

Row 3: k2, *yo, k3, yo,* k1, repeat between *s, k2. (15 sts)

Row 5: k2, *yo, k2tog, yo, k1, yo, ssk, yo,* k1, repeat between *s, k2. (19 sts)

Row 7: k2, *yo, k2tog, yo, k3, yo, ssk, yo,* k1, repeat between *s, k2. (23 sts)

Row 9: k2, *yo, k3, k2tog, yo, k4, yo,* k1, repeat between *s, k2. (27 sts)

Row 11: k2, *yo, k1, yo, ssk, yo, ssk, k1, k2tog, yo, k2tog, yo, k1, yo,* k1, repeat between *s, k2. (31 sts)

Row 13: k2, *yo, k3, yo, ssk, yo, sk2p, yo, k2tog, yo, k3, yo,* k1, repeat between *s, k2. (35 sts)

Row 15: k2, *yo, k2tog, yo, k1, yo, ssk, yo, ssk, k1, k2tog, yo, k2tog, yo, k1, yo, ssk, yo,* k1, repeat between *s, k2. (39 sts)

Row 17: k2, *yo, k2tog, yo, k3, yo, ssk, yo, sk2p, yo, k2tog, yo, k3, yo, ssk, yo,* k1, repeat between *s, k2. (43 sts)

Leaf Lace Beginning: (Chart 2)

Row 1: (RS) k2, *yo, k1, yo, place marker,* k1, repeat between *s, k2. (11 sts)

Row 2 and all even rows: (WS) k2, purl to last 2 sts, k2.

Row 3: k2, *yo, k3, yo,* k1, repeat between *s, k2. (15 sts)

Row 5: k2, *yo, k5, yo,* k1, repeat between *s, k2. (19 sts)

Row 7: k2, *yo, k7, yo,* k1, repeat between *s, k2. (23 sts)

Row 9: k2, *yo, k9, yo,* k1, repeat between *s, k2. (27 sts)

Row 11: k2, *yo, k1, yo, k3, sk2p, k3, yo, k1, yo,* k1, repeat between *s, k2. (31 sts)

Row 13: k2, *yo, k3, yo, k2, sk2p, k2, yo, k3, yo,* k1, repeat between *s, k2. (35 sts)

Row 15: k2, *yo, k5, yo, k1, sk2p, k1, yo, k5, yo,* k1, repeat between *s, k2. (39 sts)

Row 17: k2, *yo, k7, yo, sk2p, yo, k7, yo,* k1, repeat between *s, k2. (43 sts)

Medallion Lace Beginning: (Chart 3)

Row 1: (RS) k2, *yo, k1, yo, place marker,* k1, repeat between *s, k2. (11 sts)

Row 2 and all even rows: (WS) k2, purl to last 2 sts, k2.

Row 3: k2, *yo, k3, yo,* k1, repeat between *s, k2. (15 sts)

Row 5: k2, *yo, k5, yo,* k1, repeat between *s, k2. (19 sts)

Row 7: k2, *yo, k1, k2tog, yo, k1, yo, ssk, k1, yo,* k1, repeat between *s, k2. (23 sts)

Row 9: k2, *yo, k1, k2tog, yo, k3, yo, ssk, k1, yo,* k1, repeat between *s, k2. (27 sts)

Row 11: k2, *yo, k1, yo, ssk, k1, yo, sk2p, yo, k1, k2tog, yo, k1, yo,* k1, repeat between *s, k2. (31 sts)

Row 13: k2, *yo, k3, yo, ssk, k3, k2tog, yo, k3, yo,* k1, repeat between *s, k2. (35 sts)

Row 15: k2, *yo, k5, yo, ssk, k1, k2tog, yo, k5, yo,* k1, repeat between *s, k2. (39 sts)

Row 17: k2, *yo, k1, k2tog, yo, k1, yo, ssk, k1, yo, sk2p, yo, k1, k2tog, yo, k1, yo, ssk, k1, yo,* k1, repeat between *s, k2. (43 sts)

Ripple Lace Beginning: (Chart 4)

Row 1: (RS) k2, *yo, k1, yo, place marker,* k1, repeat between *s, k2. (11 sts)

Row 2 and all even rows: (WS) k2, purl to last 2 sts, k2.

Row 3: k2, *yo, k3, yo,* k1, repeat between *s, k2. (15 sts)

Row 5: k2, *yo, k5, yo,* k1, repeat between *s, k2. (19 sts)

Row 7: k2, *yo, k2, yo, sk2p, yo, k2, yo,* k1, repeat between *s, k2. (23 sts)

Row 9: k2, *yo, k1, yo, ssk, k3, k2tog, yo, k1, yo,* k1, repeat between *s, k2. (27 sts)

Row 11: k2, *yo, k1, yo, ssk, yo, ssk, k1, k2tog, yo, k2tog, yo, k1, yo,* k1, repeat between *s, k2. (31 sts)

Row 13: k2, *yo, k3, yo, ssk, yo, sk2p, yo, k2tog, yo, k3, yo,* k1, repeat between *s, k2. (35 sts)

Row 15: k2, *yo, k5, yo, ssk, k1, k2tog, yo, k5, yo,* k1, repeat between *s, k2. (39 sts)

Row 17: k2, *yo, k1, k2tog, yo, k1, yo, ssk, k1, yo, sk2p, yo, k1, k2tog, yo, k1, yo, ssk, k1, yo,* k1, repeat between *s, k2. (43 sts)

Lace Beginnings Charts

FLOWER LACE BEGINNING - CHART 1

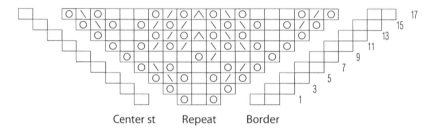

Center st   Repeat   Border

LEAF LACE BEGINNING - CHART 2

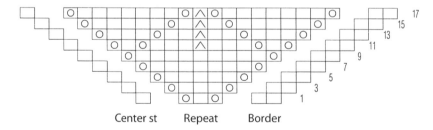

Center st   Repeat   Border

38

MEDALLION LACE BEGINNING - CHART 3

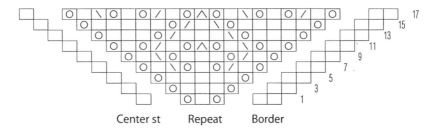

Center st   Repeat   Border

RIPPLE LACE BEGINNING - CHART 4

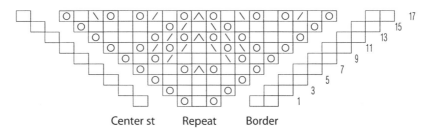

Center st   Repeat   Border

Flower Shawl -
Stockinette Flower lace
in sport weight

Lace Repeats

Notes:

1. Place a marker before the center stitch and before the last 2 border stitches.
2. Stitch count only is given for the Repeat worked immediately after the Beginning lace.
3. Transition Information shows which Transition rows should be substituted for the last four Beginning or Repeat rows before starting that lace.

Flower Lace Repeat: (10-row Repeat, Chart 5)

Transition Information:

From Leaf use Transition 4; from Medallion or Ripple use Transition 5

Row 1: (RS) k2, *yo, [k3, k2tog, yo, k5] to 9 sts before marker, k3, k2tog, yo, k4, yo,* k1, repeat between *s, k2. (47 sts)

Row 2 and all even rows: (WS) k2, purl to last 2 sts, k2.

Row 3: k2, *yo, k1, [yo, ssk, yo, ssk, k1, k2tog, yo, k2tog, yo, k1] to marker, yo,* k1, repeat between *s, k2. (51 sts)

Row 5: k2, *yo, k2, [k1, yo, ssk, yo, sk2p, yo, k2tog, yo, k2] to 1 st before marker, k1, yo,* k1, repeat between *s, k2. (55 sts)

Row 7: k2, *yo, k2tog, yo, k1, [yo, ssk, yo, ssk, k1, k2tog, yo, k2tog, yo, k1] to 2 sts before marker, yo, ssk, yo,* k1, repeat between *s, k2. (59 sts)

Row 9: k2, *yo, k2tog, yo, k2, [k1, yo, ssk, yo, sk2p, yo, k2tog, yo, k2] to 3 sts before marker, k1, yo, ssk, yo,* k1, repeat between *s, k2. (63 sts)

"Too much of a good thing can be wonderful." - Mae West

Leaf Lace Repeat: (10-row Repeat, Chart 6)

Transition Information: From Flower, Medallion or Ripple use Transition 1.

Note: Use Row A1 in place of Row 1 for a Repeat worked immediately after the Beginning lace. Use Row 1 for all other Repeats.

Row A1: (RS) k2, *yo, k4, k2tog, k3, yo, k1, yo, k3, ssk, k4, yo,* k1, repeat between *s, k2. (47 sts)

Row 1: (RS) k2, *yo, k4, k2tog, k3, yo, k1, [yo, k3, sk2p, k3, yo, k1] to 9 sts before marker, yo, k3, ssk, k4, yo,* k1, repeat between *s, k2.

Row 2 and all even rows: (WS) k2, purl to last 2 sts, k2.

Row 3: k2, *yo, k1, [yo, k3, sk2p, k3, yo, k1] to marker, yo,* k1, repeat between *s, k2. (51 sts)

Row 5: k2, *yo, k2, [k1, yo, k2, sk2p, k2, yo, k2] to 1 st before marker, k1, yo,* k1, repeat between *s, k2. (55 sts)

Row 7: k2, *yo, k3, [k2, yo, k1, sk2p, k1, yo, k3] to 2 sts before marker, k2, yo,* k1, repeat between *s, k2. (59 sts)

Row 9: k2, *yo, k4, [k3, yo, sk2p, yo, k4] to 3 sts before marker, k3, yo,* k1, repeat between *s, k2. (63 sts)

Medallion Lace Repeat: (10-row Repeat, Chart 7)

Transition Information: From Flower use Transition 2; from Leaf use Transition 3; from Ripple no Transition is needed.

Row 1: (RS) k2, *yo, k1, k2tog, yo, k2, [k1, yo, ssk, yo, sk2p, yo, k2tog, yo, k2] to 4 sts before marker, k1, yo, ssk, k1, yo,* k1, repeat between *s, k2. (47 sts)

Row 2 and all even rows: (WS) k2, purl to last 2 sts, k2.

Row 3: k2, *yo, k1, [yo, ssk, k1, yo, sk2p, yo, k1, k2tog, yo, k1] to marker, yo,* k1, repeat between *s, k2. (51 sts)

Row 5: k2, *yo, k3, [yo, ssk, k3, k2tog, yo, k3] to marker, yo,* k1, repeat between *s, k2. (55 sts)

Row 7: k2, *yo, k5, [yo, ssk, k1, k2tog, yo, k5] to marker, yo,* k1, repeat between *s, k2. (59 sts)

Row 9: k2, *yo, k1, [k2tog, yo, k1, yo, ssk, k1, yo, sk2p, yo, k1] to 6 sts before marker, k2tog, yo, k1, yo, ssk, k1, yo,* k1, repeat between *s, k2. (63 sts)

Ripple Lace Repeat: (20-row Repeat, Chart 8)

Transition Information: From Flower use Transition 2; from Leaf use Transition 3; from Medallion no Transition is necessary.

Row 1: (RS) k2, *yo, k1, k2tog, yo, k2, [k1, yo, ssk, k3, k2tog, yo, k2] to 4 sts before marker, k1, yo, ssk, k1, yo,* k1, repeat between *s, k2. (47 sts)

Row 2 and all even rows: (WS) k2, purl to last 2 sts, k2.

Row 3: k2, *yo, k1, k2tog, yo, k2tog, yo, k1 [yo, ssk, yo, ssk, k1, k2tog, yo, k2tog, yo, k1] to 5 sts before marker, yo, ssk, yo, ssk, k1, yo,* k1, repeat between *s, k2. (51 sts)

Row 5: k2, *yo, k1, k2tog, yo, k2tog, yo, k2, [k1, yo, ssk, yo, sk2p, yo, k2tog, yo, k2] to 6 sts before marker, k1, yo, ssk, yo, ssk, k1, yo,* k1, repeat between *s, k2. (55 sts)

Row 7: k2, *yo, k3, k2tog, yo, k3, [k2, yo, ssk, k1, k2tog, yo, k3] to 7 sts before marker, k2, yo, ssk, k3, yo,* k1, repeat between *s, k2. (59 sts)

Row 9: k2, *yo, k2, yo, sk2p, yo, k1, k2tog, yo, k1, [yo, ssk, k1, yo, sk2p, yo, k1, k2tog, yo, k1] to 8 sts before marker, yo, ssk, k1, yo, sk2p, yo, k2, yo,* k1, repeat between *s, k2. (63 sts)

Row 11: k2, *yo, [k1, yo, ssk, k3, k2tog, yo, k2] to 9 sts before marker, k1, yo, ssk, k3, k2tog, yo, k1, yo,* k1, repeat between *s, k2. (67 sts)

Row 13: k2, *yo, k1, [yo, ssk, yo, ssk, k1, k2tog, yo, k2tog, yo, k1] to marker, yo,* k1, repeat between *s, k2. (71 sts)

Row 15: k2, *yo, k2, [k1, yo, ssk, yo, sk2p, yo, k2tog, yo, k2] to 1 st before marker, k1, yo,* k1, repeat between *s, k2. (75 sts)

Row 17: k2, *yo, k3, [k2, yo, ssk, k1, k2tog, yo, k3] to 2 sts before marker, k2, yo,* k1, repeat between *s, k2. (79 sts)

Row 19: k2, *yo, k1, k2tog, yo, k1, [yo, ssk, k1, yo, sk2p, yo, k1, k2tog, yo, k1] to 3 sts before marker, yo, ssk, k1, yo,* k1, repeat between *s, k2. (83 sts)

FLOWER LACE REPEAT - CHART 5

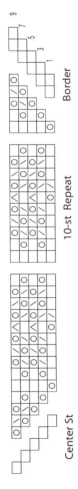

LEAF LACE REPEAT - CHART 6

(No Transition needed to Edging)
Work rows 1 through 10 only after an 18-row Beginning. Work rows 11 through 20 for all other Repeats.

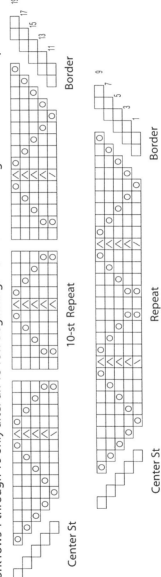

MEDALLION LACE REPEAT - CHART 7
(No Transition needed to Ripple lace)

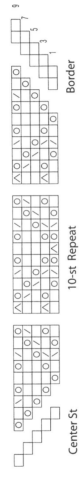

Border

10-st Repeat

Center St

RIPPLE LACE REPEAT - CHART 8
(No transition needed to Medallion lace)

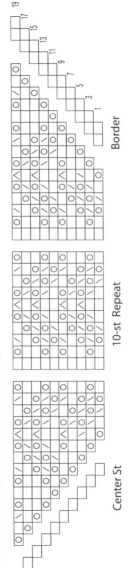

Border

10-st Repeat

Center St

45

Lace Transitions

Transition I: (Chart 9)
Use when going from Flower, Medallion or Ripple to Leaf lace or Edging.
Row 1: (RS) k2, *yo, k3, [k2, yo, ssk, k1, k2tog, yo, k3] to 2 sts before marker, k2, yo,* k1, repeat between *s, k2.
Rows 2 & 4: (WS): k2, purl to last 2 sts, k2.
Row 3: k2, *yo, k4, [k3, yo, sk2p, yo, k4] to 3 sts before marker, k3, yo,* k1, repeat between *s, k2.

Transition 2: (Chart 10)
Use when going from Flower to Ripple or Medallion lace.
Row 1: (RS) k2, *yo, k3, [k2, yo, ssk, k1, k2tog, yo, k3] to 2 sts before marker, k2, yo,* k1, repeat between *s, k2.
Rows 2 & 4: (WS) k2, purl to last 2 sts, k2.
Row 3: k2, *yo, k1, k2tog, yo, k1, [yo, ssk, k1, yo, sk2p, yo, k1, k2tog, yo, k1] to 3 sts before marker, yo, ssk, k1, yo,* k1, repeat between *s, k2.

Transition 3: (Chart 11)
Use when going from Leaf to Medallion or Ripple lace.
Row 1: (RS) k2, *yo, k3, [k2, yo, k1, sk2p, k1, yo, k3] to 2 sts before marker, k2, yo,* k1, repeat between *s, k2.
Rows 2 & 4: (WS) k2, purl to last 2 sts, k2.
Row 3: k2, *yo, k1, k2tog, yo, k1, [yo, ssk, k1, yo, sk2p, yo, k1, k2tog, yo, k1] to 3 sts before marker, yo, ssk, k1, yo,* k1, repeat between *s, k2.

Transition 4: (Chart 12)

Use when going from Leaf to Flower lace.

Row 1: (RS) k2, *yo, k2tog, yo, k1, [yo, ssk, yo, k1, sk2p, k1, yo, k2tog, yo, k1] to 2 sts before marker, yo, ssk, yo,* k1, repeat between *s, k2.

Rows 2 & 4 (WS): k2, purl to last 2 sts, k2.

Row 3: k2, *yo, k2tog, yo, k2, [k1, yo, ssk, yo, sk2p, yo, k2tog, yo, k2] to 3 sts before marker, k1, yo, ssk, yo,* k1, repeat between *s, k2.

Transition 5: (Chart 13)

Use when going from Medallion or Ripple to Flower lace.

Row 1: (RS) k2, *yo, k2tog, yo, k1, [yo, ssk, yo, ssk, k1, k2tog, yo, k2tog, yo, k1] to 2 sts before marker, yo, ssk, yo,* k1, repeat between *s, k2.

Rows 2 & 4: (WS) k2, purl to last 2 sts, k2.

Row 3: k2, *yo, k2tog, yo, k2, [k1, yo, ssk, yo, sk2p, yo, k2tog, yo, k2] to 3 sts before marker, k1, yo, ssk, yo,* k1, repeat between *s, k2.

TRANSITION 1 - CHART 9
(Use when going from Flower, Medallion or Ripple to Leaf lace or Edging)

Center St   10-st Repeat   Border

TRANSITION 2 - CHART 10
(Use when going from Flower to Ripple or Medallion lace)

Center St   10-st Repeat   Border

TRANSITION 3 - CHART 11
(Use when going from Leaf to Medallion or Ripple lace)

Center St   10-st Repeat   Border

TRANSITION 4 - CHART 12
(Use when going from Leaf to Flower lace)

Center St   10-st Repeat   Border

TRANSITION 5 - CHART 13
(Use when going from Medallion or Ripple to Flower lace)

Center St   10-st Repeat   Border

Garden Shawl -
Stockinette Ripple, Medallion, Flower and Leaf lace
in lace weight

Edging

After working desired number of Repeats for the body of the triangle, it is time to start the Edging. Leaf lace can be worked until the end of the Repeat. For Flower, Medallion and Ripple lace, substitute Transition 1 for the last 4 rows of the Repeat. After the Transition is worked, the stitch count will remain even until the scallop increases in Row 7.

Edging: (Chart 14)
Notes:
1. Edging rows are worked to last border st instead of to center st.
2. No increases are worked until Row 7.
3. Options for including 1 or 3 beads per scallop are given in Row 8.
To bead a stitch, place it back on the holding needle, then insert crochet hook through bead and pull the stitch through bead. Place beaded stitch on working needle.

Rows 1, 3 & 5: k2, *yo, k3, sk2p, k3, yo, k1,* repeat to last st, k1.
Rows 2, 4 & 6: k2, purl to last 2 sts, k2.
Row 7: k2, *yo, k9, yo, k1,* repeat to last st, k1.

•Row 8A (without beads): Knit.

•Row 8B (with 1 bead per scallop): k2, place last st back onto holding needle and bead it, k11, *knit and bead 1 st, k11,* repeat to last 2 sts, knit and bead 1 st, k1.

•Row 8C (with 3 beads per scallop): k2, place last st back onto holding needle and bead it, knit and bead next st, k9, *knit and bead 3 sts, k9,* repeat to last 3 sts, knit and bead next 2 sts, k1.
Note: Only 2 sts are beaded on beginning and ending borders.

Edging - Chart 14

Notes:

1. Repeat is worked across all sts to final border st.
2. See written instructions for Row 8 and cast-off information.

End Border   10-st Repeat   Beginning Border

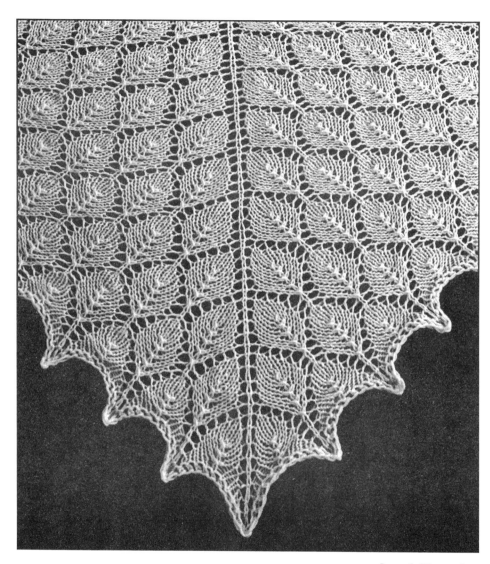

Leaf Shawl -
Stockinette Leaf lace
in sport weight

Casting Off

For the edging to scallop, the cast-off must be worked at a moderate to loose tension. The looser the cast-off, the more elongated the scallops will be. The Elastic Cast-off described below creates an edge with a little extra thickness. To test whether it is loose enough, stretch the edging after casting off for a few inches. The edging should form peaks at the beaded or "yo, k1, yo" sts and valleys above the decreases. If the edging does not naturally scallop, work the cast-off more loosely. If the scallops are more elongated than preferred, work the cast-off less loosely.

Elastic Cast-off -
k1, *k1, transfer the 2 sts back to holding needle and k2tog through back loops,* repeat between *s across.

Finishing

Weave in yarn ends, but wait until piece is blocked and dry to trim them.

Blocking -

Lace often looks limp and lumpy when it comes off the needles, and blocking is the simple process that brings out its beauty. How heavily the lace is blocked is a personal preference. A shawl can simply be smoothed into shape or severely stretched. Either way, it will become larger, and garter stitch lace can grow up to 30 percent. However, yarns have a maximum they will stretch, so shawls that are heavily blocked often will relax a bit afterwards.

Triangles can be blocked and pinned onto any flat surface, including carpeted floors or a mattress. A blocking board, or insulation board covered with fabric, can be placed on a table for blocking and then propped against a wall for drying.

In addition to a basin of water and wool soap (or a steamer or steam iron), the only tools needed are a tape measure and rustproof pins. Blocking wires are optional, but very handy for light-weight shawls since they make it easy to create a straight top edge. Shawls in heavier yarns simply can be smoothed into shape across the top edge, and then the points can be pinned.

Wet Blocking -

To wet block, fill a basin with lukewarm water and a tiny amount of wool soap if desired. Soak the lace for at least 20 minutes to saturate the yarn. Supporting the wet piece, gently squeeze out the water, and rinse by immersing in clean water of the same temperature. Again, support the piece and gently squeeze out the water. Roll it up in a towel to blot out more moisture.

Lay triangle out flat, and smooth into shape. If using blocking wires, run through eyelets along top edge and pin in place. Use a tape measure to make sure each side has been pulled out the same distance from the center stitch.

Then smooth out the center point the same distance and pin. Pin out evenly along side edges at each scallop point.

Leave shawl pinned in place until thoroughly dry. Then unpin, and trim yarn ends.

Steam Blocking -

Spread out the triangle on a flat surface. Hold steamer several inches above the piece and gently steam entire surface. Smooth into shape and pin out points as described above.

Acrylic yarns must be heavily steamed or the built-in memory will pull the scallops out of the blocked shape. Steam acrylic yarns carefully since the new memory created for the yarn will be permanent. Leave in place until thoroughly dry. Then unpin and trim yarn ends.

"There's a time when what you're creating and the environment you're creating it in come together." - Grace Hartigan

Final Thoughts

I hope this book has launched a new creative journey for you. Lace knitting can be addictive, and there are many ways to experiment with triangles. Stitch dictionaries and lace designs are great resources for other motifs and other shapes.

To track your journey, it is fun to keep a knitting journal. Record the type of yarn, needle size and what you liked or didn't like about each design you knit. This documents your personal knitting style and provides a quick, useful reference when considering new projects.

The knitting world is broad and offers many paths to explore and friends to discover. As you travel through it, I hope it enriches your life as it has mine.

"The world is round, and the place that may seem like the end may also be the beginning."
- Ivy Baker Priest

Rose Ribbons Shawl -
Stockinette Flower and Leaf lace with
no transitions except before edging
in fingering weight

Appendix

Size and Yardage Chart - Page I

Rows-to-Edging	88	98*	108	118*	128	138*
Stitch Count to Edging	183	203	223	243	263	283
Final Stitch Count	219	243	267	291	315	339

*Numbers that can be used for Ripple-only lace triangles

Blocked Size
Depth at center x top width in inches. For centimeters, multiply inches by 2.54.
(Use size as general guideline since yarns vary in elasticity.)

Lace Weight (18+ wpi)	19½ x 39	21 x 42	22½ x 45	24 x 48	25½ x 51	27 x 54
Fingering Weight (16-17 wpi)	20½ x 41	22 x 44	24 x 48	26 x 52	27½ x 55	29 x 58
Shetland/Sport/dk (13-15 wpi)	24 x 48	26 x 52	28 x 56	30 x 60	32 x 64	36 x 72
Worsted Weight (11-12 wpi)	30 x 60	33 x 66	36 x 72	39 x 78	42 x 84	45 x 90

Yardage Required
To convert to meters multiply yardage given by .914.

Lace Weight	195	240	295	345	410	475
Fingering Weight	230	285	345	415	485	565
Shetland/Sport/dk	275	340	410	490	575	665
Worsted Weight	430	530	640	765	900	1040

Beads Required

1 per scallop	19	21	23	25	27	29
3 per scallop	55	61	67	73	79	85

Size and Yardage Chart - Page 2

Rows-to-Edging	148	158*	168	178*	188	198*
Stitch Count to Edging	303	323	343	363	383	403
Final Stitch Count	363	387	411	435	459	483

*Numbers that can be used for Ripple-only lace triangles

Blocked Size
Depth at center x top width in inches. For centimeters, multiply inches by 2.54.
(Use size as general guideline since yarns vary in elasticity.)

Lace Weight (18+ wpi)	28½ x 57	30 x 60	31½ x 63	33 x 66	34½ x 69	36 x 72
Fingering Weight (16-17 wpi)	31 x 62	33 x 66	34½ x 9	36 x 72	38 x 76	40 x 80
Shetland/Sport/dk (13-15 wpi)	38 x 76	40 x 80	43 x 86	45 x 90	48 x 96	50 x 100
Worsted Weight (11-12 wpi)	48 x 96	51 x 102	54 x 108	57 x 114	60 x 120	63 x 126

Yardage Required
To convert to meters multiply yardage given by .914.

Lace Weight	545	620	670	785	875	990
Fingering Weight	645	735	830	935	1040	1175
Shetland/Sport/dk	765	870	985	1105	1230	1390
Worsted Weight	1195	1365	1540	1725	1925	2175

Beads Required

1 per scallop	31	33	35	37	39	41
3 per scallop	91	97	103	109	115	121

Ripple Shawl -
Stockinette Ripple lace
in sport weight

Sample Shawls

Following is information on the sample shawls in this book. Sizes shown are the relaxed size after blocking.

"Art is a vehicle not just for beauty, but for all the possibilities of things people have inside."
- Gale Jackson

Single-Lace Triangles

Only one lace was used on each of these shawls. Transition rows were worked before the Edging except on the Leaf shawl where no Transition was needed.

Leaf Shawl - page 52

Beginning	18 rows
10-row Repeat - 9x	<u>90 rows</u>
Total Rows-to-Edging	108 rows

Yarn: 410 yds (375m) sport weight yarn (14 wpi)
Sample shawl used 3 - 50g skeins Naturally Haven 4 Ply
Needle Size: US 6 (4mm)
Gauge: 18 sts = 4" (10cm) in stockinette stitch
Finished Size: 25" (63.5cm) deep and 50" (127cm) wide

Medallion or Flower Shawls - pages 8 and 40

Beginning	18 rows
10-row Repeat - 9x	
including Transition #1	<u>90 rows</u>
Total Rows-to-Edging	108 Rows

Yarn: 410 yds (375m) sport weight yarn (14 wpi)
Each sample shawl used 3 - 50g skeins Naturally Haven 4 Ply
Needle Size: US 6 (4mm)
Gauge: 18 sts = 4" (10cm) in stockinette stitch
Finished Size: 25" (63.5cm) deep and 50" (127cm) wide

Ripple Shawl - page 62

Beginning	18 rows
20-row Repeat - 5x	
including Transition #1	100 rows
Total Rows-to-Edging	118 rows

Yarn: 490 yds (448m) sport weight yarn (14 wpi)
Sample shawl used 3 - 50g skeins Naturally Haven 4 Ply
Needle Size: US 6 (4mm)
Gauge: 18 sts = 4" (10cm) in stockinette stitch
Finished Size: 27" (60cm) deep and 54" (137cm) wide

Two-Lace Triangles

Rose Ribbons Shawl - page 57

This stockinette stitch triangle shows off the ribbon effect that occurs when Transition rows are not worked between changing lace patterns. Two Repeats of Flower lace alternate with 2 Repeats of Leaf lace on this triangle. Transition rows are used only before the Edging.

Flower Beginning	18 rows
Flower Repeat	10 rows
*10-row Leaf Repeat - 2 x	20 rows
10-row Flower Repeat - 2 x	20 rows
Repeat from * once more	
including Transition #1	<u>40 rows</u>
Total Rows-to-Edging	108 rows

Yarn: 345 yds (315m) fingering weight (17 wpi)
Sample shawl used 2 - 50g skeins of Frog Tree Alpaca fingering weight
Needles: US 5 (3.75mm)
Gauge: 19 sts = 4" (10cm) in stockinette stitch
Finished Size: 24" (61cm) deep and 48" (122cm) wide

Sand Dollar Shawl - page 23

Medallion and Ripple lace alternate on this stockinette stitch shawl.
It has 1 bead on each Edging scallop.
No Transition needed until the Edging.

Medallion Beginning	18 rows
20-row Ripple Repeat	
+ 10-Row Medallion Repeat - 3x	
including Transition 1	<u>90 rows</u>
Total Rows-to-Edging	108 rows

Yarn: 640 yds (585m) worsted weight (11 wpi)
Sample shawl used 2 - 200g skeins of Natural Wool 8 Ply
Needle Size: US 9 (5.5mm)
Gauge: 12 sts = 4" (10cm) in stockinette stitch
Beads: 23
Finished Size: 36" (91cm) deep and 72" (183cm) wide

Three-Lace Triangle

Sunshine and Shadows Shawl- page 24

Medallion and Leaf lace alternate to a Ripple border on this garter stitch triangle. Transition rows are used throughout.

Medallion Beginning	
including Transition 1	18 rows
*Leaf Repeat	
including Transition 3	10 rows
Medallion Repeat	
including Transition 1	10 rows
Repeat from * 2 more times, ending with	
Medallion Repeat	
no Transition needed	40 rows
Ripple Repeat	
including Transition 1	<u>20 rows</u>
Total Rows-to-Edging	98 rows

Yarn: 285 yds (261m) fingering weight (16 wpi)
Sample shawl used 2 - 50 gram skeins of Frog Tree Suri Alpaca fingering weight
Needles: US 6 (4mm)
Gauge: 15 sts = 4" (10cm) in stockinette stitch
Finished Size: 26" (66cm) deep and 52" (132cm) wide

Four-Lace Triangle

Garden Shawl - page 49

All four lace patterns are combined on this stockinette stitch triangle. It has 3 beads at each Edging scallop. Transition rows are used as shown.

Ripple Beginning	18 rows
Ripple Repeat	20 rows
10-row Medallion Repeat - 3x	
including Transition #5	30 rows
10-row Flower Repeat - 3x	
including Transition #1	30 rows
10-row Leaf Repeat - 2x	<u>20 rows</u>
Total Rows-to-Edging	118 rows

Yarn: 345 yds (315m) lace weight (22 wpi)
Sample shawl used 1.1 ounce of Jaggerspun Zephyr
Needle Size: US 4 (3.5mm)
Gauge: 24 sts = 4" (10cm) in stockinette stitch
Beads: 73
Finished Size: 24" (61cm) deep and 48" (122cm) wide

Special Thanks -

I feel fortunate to live in a time with so many wonderful knitting resources and am especially grateful to these authors whose books continue to inspire me: Mary Walker Phillips, Margaret Stove, Meg Swansen, Barbara Walker, Martha Waterman and Elizabeth Zimmermann

Special thanks to Bev Galeskas who suggested this project and Karen Aho who has enthusiastically supported my work from the early days.

Also, I'd like to thank my long-time knitting buddies Wilma Bishop, Jacque Blix, Jody Grage and Mary Lou Johnson who never ask why I'm working on another shawl.

About the Author -

Evelyn Clark is a designer who lives in the Pacific Northwest. She left a marketing career to live a simpler life and developed a passion for putting holes in her knitting. Her designs have been published by Fiber Trends, Interweave Press, Knitter's, Leisure Arts and Vogue.

"Life is entirely too time-consuming." - Irene Peter